YELLOWSTONE
NATIONAL PARK
ACTIVITY BOOK

NATIONAL PARKS ACTIVITIES SERIES

YELLOWSTONE NATIONAL PARK ACTIVITY BOOK

Copyright 2021
Published by Little Bison Press

The author acknowledges that the land on which Yellowstone National Park is located are the traditional lands of the Assiniboine and Sioux, Blackfeet, Cheyenne River Sioux, Coeur d'Alene, Comanche, Colville Reservation, Crow, Crow Creek Sioux, Eastern Shoshone, Flandreau Santee Sioux, Gros Ventre and Assiniboine, Kiowa, Little Shell Chippewa, Lower Brule Sioux, Nez Perce, Northern Arapaho, Northern Cheyenne, Oglala Sioux, Rosebud Sioux, Salish and Kootenai, Shoshone-Bannock, Sisseton Wahpeton, Spirit Lake, Standing Rock Sioux, Turtle Mountain Band of the Chippewa, Umatilla Reservation, Yankton Sioux.

LITTLE BISON

Press

For more free national parks activities, visit
Littlebisonpress.com

About Yellowstone National Park

Yellowstone National Park is notable for many reasons. Most of the park is located in the state of Wyoming, but it also includes parts of Idaho and Montana. Yellowstone was made the first national park in the United States in 1872, but it was also the first national park in the world.

This park is famous for its hydrothermal features. There are geysers, hot springs, mudpots, and fumaroles. Over half of the world's geysers are located here. Geyers are a type of hot spring that is under pressure and erupts, sending jets of water and steam into the air. Old Faithful is one of the most popular geysers in the park. It erupts on a predictable schedule.

Visitors can view wildlife in Yellowstone National Park. Bison, bears, wolves, and many other animals live in areas in and around the park. If you see them, make sure to give them space!

Yellowstone National Park is famous for:
- being the first national park in the world
- hydrothermal features
- amazing wildlife

Hey! I'm Parker!

I'm the only snail in history to visit every National Park in the United States! Come join me on my adventures in Yellowstone National Park.

Throughout this book, we will learn about the history of the park, the animals and plants that live here, and things to do here if you ever get to visit in person. This book is also full of games and activities!

Last but not least, I am hidden 9 times on different pages. See how many times you can find me. This page doesn't count!

Yellowstone Bingo

Let's play bingo! Cross off each box that you are able to during your visit to the national park. Try to get a bingo down, across, or diagonally. If you can't visit the park, use the bingo board to plan your perfect trip.

Pick out some activities that you would want to do during your visit. What would you do first? How long would you spend there? What animals would you try to see?

SPOT A BISON	SEE A GEYSER	IDENTIFY A TREE	TAKE A PICTURE AT AN OVERLOOK	WATCH A MOVIE AT THE VISITORS CENTER
GO FOR A HIKE	LEARN ABOUT THE INDIGENOUS PEOPLE THAT LIVE IN THIS AREA	WITNESS A SUNRISE OR SUNSET	OBSERVE THE NIGHT SKIES	SMELL A MUDPOT
HEAR A BIRD CALL	SEE A RAINBOW HOTSPRING	FREE SPACE	GO FOR A DIP IN THE BOILING RIVER	VISIT A RANGER STATION
PICK UP TEN PIECES OF TRASH	GO CAMPING	SEE AN ELK	WALK ON A BOARDWALK	SPOT A BIRD OF PREY
LEARN ABOUT SAFE WILDLIFE VIEWING	SEE THE YELLOWSTONE LODGE	HAVE A PICNIC	SPOT SOME ANIMAL TRACKS	PARTICIPATE IN A RANGER-LED ACTIVITY

The National Park Logo

The National Park System has over 400 units in the US. Just like Yellowstone National Park, each location is unique or special in some way. The areas include other national parks, historic sites, monuments, seashores, and other recreation areas.

Each element of the National Park emblem represents something that the National Park Service protects. Fill in each blank below to show what each symbol represents.

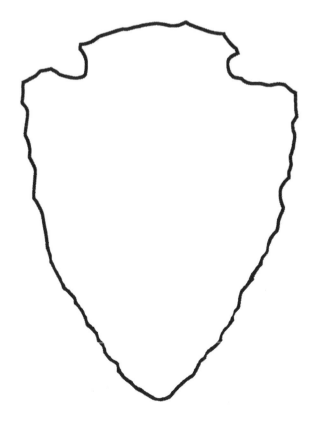

WORD BANK:
MOUNTAINS, ARROWHEAD, BISON, SEQUOIA TREE, WATER

This represents all plants. _____

This represents all animals. _____

This symbol represents the landscapes. _____

This represents the waters protected by the park service. _____

This represents the historical and archeological values. _____

Now it's your turn! Pretend you are designing a new national park. Add elements to the design that represent the things that your park protects

What is the name of your park?

Describe why you included the symbols that you included. What do they mean?

Things to Do Jumble

Unscramble the letters to uncover activities you can do while in Yellowstone National Park. Hint: each one ends in -ing.

1. NIBOTAG
   ☐☐☐☐ ING

2. KHINIG
   ☐☐☐ ING

3. IRDGNIB
   ☐☐☐☐ ING

4. NMAGICP
   ☐☐☐☐ ING

5. KINNICIPCG
   ☐☐☐☐☐☐☐ ING

6. EINSSTEIGHG
   ☐☐☐☐☐☐☐☐ ING

7. SHOSNINGOWE
   ☐☐☐☐☐☐☐ ING

Word Bank

birding
reading
camping
snowshoeing
boating
hiking
hunting
singing
yelling
sightseeing
picnicking

Making a Difference

It is important to protect the valuable resources of the world, not just beautiful places like national parks.

How many of these things do you do at home? If you answered "no" to more than 10 items, talk to the grownups in your life to see if there are any household habits you might be able to change. Conserving our collective resources helps us all.

Yes	No	Do you…
☐	☐	turn off the water when you are brushing your teeth?
☐	☐	use LED light bulbs when possible?
☐	☐	use a reusable water bottle instead of disposable ones?
☐	☐	ride your bike or take the bus instead of riding in the car?
☐	☐	have a rain barrel under your roof gutters to collect rain water?
☐	☐	take quick showers?
☐	☐	avoid putting more food on your plate than you will eat?
☐	☐	take reusable lunch containers?
☐	☐	grow a garden?
☐	☐	buy items with less packaging?
☐	☐	recycle paper?
☐	☐	recycle plastic?
☐	☐	have a compost pile at home so you can make your own soil?
☐	☐	pick up trash when you see it on the trail?
☐	☐	plan a "staycation" and fly only when you have to?

# of Yes	# of No

Add up your score! Are there any "no"s that you want to turn into a yes?

Can you think of any other ways to protect our natural resources?

Go Birdwatching at Swan Lake Flatts

start here

DID YOU KNOW?
Yellowstone National Park is home to several birds of prey, including eagles, ospreys, and owls. Birds of prey are birds that hunt other animals for food.

Bird Scavenger Hunt

Yellowstone National Park is a great place to go birdwatching. You don't have to be able to identify different species of birds in order to have fun. Open your eyes and tune in your ears. Check off as many birds on this list as you can.

- ☐ A colorful bird
- ☐ A brown bird
- ☐ A bird in a tree
- ☐ A bird with long tail feathers
- ☐ A bird making noise
- ☐ A bird eating or hunting
- ☐ A bird with spots

- ☐ A big bird
- ☐ A small bird
- ☐ A hopping bird
- ☐ A flying bird
- ☐ A bird's nest
- ☐ A bird's footprint on the ground
- ☐ A bird with stripes somewhere on it

What was the easiest bird on the list to find? What was the hardest?
Why do you think that was?

_____

_____

_____

Yellowstone National Park

Date: _____

Season: _____

Who I went with: _____

Which entrance: _____

How was your experience? Write a few sentences on your trip. Where did you stay? What did you do? What was your favorite activity? If you have not yet visited the park, write a paragraph pretending that you did.

_____

_____

_____

_____

_____

STAMPS

Many national parks and monuments have cancellation stamps for visitors to use. These rubber stamps record the date and the location that you visited. Many people collect the markings as a free souvenir. Check with a ranger to see where you can find a stamp during your visit. If you aren't able to find one, you can draw your own.

Where is the Park?

Yellowstone National Park is in the northwest United States. It is located in mostly in Wyoming, but also in Montana and Idaho.

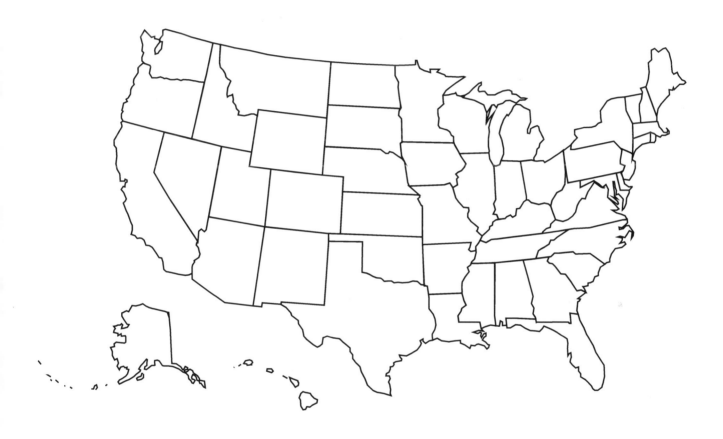

Montana, Idaho, and Wyoming

Look at the shape of Wyoming, Montana, and Idaho. Can you find them on the map? If you are from the US, can you find your home state? Color Montana blue, Idaho green, and Wyoming red. Put a star on the map where you live.

Connect the Dots

Connect the dots to figure out what this tiny critter is. There are three types of these that live in Yellowstone National Park.

Their heart rate can reach as high as 1,260 beats per minute and a breathing rate of 250 breaths per minute. Have you ever measured your breathing rate? Ask a friend or family member to set a timer for 60 seconds. Once they say "go", try to breathe normally. Count each breath until they say "stop." How do your breaths per minute compare to hummingbirds?

_____

_____

Badgers are common in Yellowstone National Park. They are well adapted to digging.

Yellowstone is the only place in the lower 48 states to continuously have a bison population roaming the landscape since prehistoric times.

Who lives here?

Here are seven animals that live in the park.
Use the word bank to fill in the clues below.

WORD BANK: WESTERN TOAD, PYGMY OWL, RIVER OTTER, MOOSE,
BISON, BADGER, GOLDEN EAGLE

⬜⬜⬜ G ⬜⬜   ⬜⬜

⬜⬜⬜⬜ E ⬜⬜ ⬛ ⬜⬜⬜⬜

⬜⬜⬜⬜ Y ⬛ ⬜⬜⬜

⬜⬜ S ⬜⬜

⬜⬜⬜⬜ E ⬜ ⬛ ⬜⬜⬜⬜

⬜⬜⬜⬜ R ⬛ ⬜⬜⬜⬜

⬜⬜⬜ S ⬜

Porcupines are well known for their defense mechanism, their quills! If attacked, these quills easily detach from the porcupine's back to pierce potential predators.

Beavers are the largest North American rodent.

Common Names
vs.
Scientific Names

A common name of an organism is a name that is based on everyday language. You have heard the common names of plants, animals, and other living things on tv, in books, and at school. Common names can also be referred to as "English" names, popular names, or farmer's name. Common names can vary from place to place. The word for a particular tree may be one thing, but that same tree has a different name in another country. Common names can even vary from region to region, even in the same country.

Scientific names, or Latin names, are given to organisms to make it possible to have uniform names for the same species. Scientific names are in Latin. You may have heard plants or animals referred to by their scientific name, or at least parts of their scientific names. Latin names are also called "binomial nomenclature" which refers to a two-part naming system. The first part of the name - the generic name -names the genus to which the species belongs. The second part of the name, the specific name, identifies the species. For example, Tyrannosaurus rex is an example of a widely known scientific name.

American Black Bear

Ursus americanus

COMMON NAME

Elk

Cervus canadensis

LATIN NAME = GENUS + SPECIES

Elk = Cervus canadensis

Black Bear = Ursus americanus

Find the Match!
Common Names and Latin Names

Match the common name to the scientific name for each animal. The first one is done for you. Use clues on the page before and after this one to complete the matches.

Elk — Haliaeetus leucocephalus

Common Juniper — Ursus americanus

Douglas Fir — Bison bison

American Black Bear — Canis lupis

Great Horned Owl — Juniperus communis

Bald Eagle — Charina bottae

Bison — Bubo virginianus

Wolf — Cervus canadensis

Rubber Boa — Pseudotsuga menziesii

Bald Eagle

Haliaeetus leucocephalus

Wolf
Canis Lupis

Bald Eagle
Haliaeetus leucocephalus

Great Horned Owl
Bubo virginianus

**Some plants
and animals
that live at
Yellowstone**

Common Juniper
Juniperus communis

Bison
Bison bison

Rubber Boa
Charina bottae

Camping Packing List

What should you take with you camping? Pretend you are in charge of your family camping trip. Make a list of what you would need to be safe and comfortable on an overnight excursion. Some considerations are listed on the side.

1.
2.
3.
4.
5.
6.
7.
8.
9.
10.
11.
12.
13.
14.
15.
16.

- What will you eat at every meal?

- What will the weather be like?

- Where will you sleep?

- What will you do during your free time?

- How luxurious do you want camp to be?

- How will you cook?

- How will you see at night?

- How will you dispose of trash?

- What might you need in case of emergencies?

The Ten Essentials

The ten essentials is a list of things that are important to have when you go for longer hikes. If you go on a hike to the <u>backcountry</u>, it is especially important that you have everything you need in case of an emergency. If you get lost or something unforeseen happens, it is good to be prepared to survive until help finds you.

The ten essentials list was developed in the 1930s by an outdoors group called the Mountaineers. Over time and technological advancements, this list has evolved. Can you identify all the things on the current list? Circle each of the "essentials" and cross out everything that doesn't make the cut.

fire: matches, lighter, tinder and/or stove	a pint of milk	extra money	headlamp plus extra batteries	extra clothes
extra water	a dog	Polaroid camera	bug net	lightweight games, like a deck of cards
extra food	a roll of duct tape	shelter	sun protection like sunglasses, sun-protective clothes and sunscreen	knife: plus a gear repair kit
a mirror	navigation: map, compass, altimeter, GPS device, or satellite messenger	first aid kit	extra flip-flops	entertainment like video games or books

Backcountry- a remote undeveloped rural area.

Bear Aware

Bears in the wild have plenty of things to eat! When you are in bear country, it is especially important to keep bears safe by making sure they can't eat any human food. When you are camping, you should store your food in special bear boxes. These metal storage boxes are animal-proof and will prevent wildlife from getting to your food.

Draw a line from each item to either the bear (if it is safe for bears to eat it) or to the bear box (if it needs to be stored.)

21

Color Old Faithful

Old Faithful is one of almost 500 geysers in Yellowstone National Park.
Geysers and other thermal features are signs of volcanic activity
beneath the surface of the earth.

LISTEN CAREFULLY

Visitors to Yellowstone National Park may hear different noises from those they hear at home. Try this activity to experience this for yourself!

First, find a place outside where it is comfortable to sit or stand for a few minutes. You can do this by yourself or with a friend or family member. Once you have a good spot, close your eyes and listen. Be quiet for one minute and pay attention to what you are hearing. List some of the sounds you have heard in one of the two boxes below:

NATURAL SOUNDS
MADE BY ANIMALS, TREES OR PLANTS, THE WIND, ETC

HUMAN-MADE SOUNDS
MADE BY PEOPLE, MACHINES, ETC

ONCE YOU ARE BACK AT HOME, TRY REPEATING YOUR EXPERIMENT:

NATURAL SOUNDS
MADE BY ANIMALS, TREES OR PLANTS, THE WIND, ETC

HUMAN-MADE SOUNDS
MADE BY PEOPLE, MACHINES, ETC

WHERE DID YOU HEAR MORE NATURAL SOUNDS? _____

WHERE DID YOU HEAR MORE HUMAN SOUNDS? _____

Listen to the world around you...

Find a dry piece of ground free of animal poop. Lie on your back and shut your eyes. Make a fist. Every time you hear a sound, put on finger up. When you have 5 fingers up, make a list of all the things you heard.

_____

_____

_____

_____

_____

Review your list. Circle the sounds the belong in the wilderness. Put an X through the ones that don't.

Stop and smell the roses...

Use your nose! Find three things in the park that smell good and three that smell bad. List the things you smelled below.

Good	Bad
_____	_____
_____	_____
_____	_____

Review your list. Circle the sounds the belong in the wilderness. Put an X through the ones that don't.

Yellowstone Word Search

Words may be horizontal, vertical, or diagonal
and they might be backward!

1. Old Faithful
2. squirrel
3. coyote
4. Roosevelt Arch
5. mud pots
6. Montana
7. geyser
8. Wyoming
9. Idaho
10. bison
11. boardwalk
12. Boiling River
13. hot spring
14. lodge
15. camping
16. wolves
17. travertine
18. hydrothermal

```
H M R E G N I M O Y W O M D M
E Y I E P W A T O R O R O A R
O L D F A I T H F U L I N G O
S O H R O D I C L T V B T H O
A D E C O Y O T E S E P A G S
V G D S L T G H B I S O N E E
P E P O V E H S B G T A A N V
E L M A R Y O E E T E T I R E
R T P T M O T Y R R E L W C L
K S Y U H E S R T M N A S A T
L G R A F E P D R C A N T M A
A N D H R F R G R K H L O P R
W I E W I A I O I F T I P I C
D P B H R S N N A M C D N H
R M N L E R G D S C T N U G O
A S Q U I R R E L E R A M E N
O C R T R A V E R T I N E W D
B O I L I N G R I V E R A D M
```

25

Find the Match!
What are Baby Animals Called?

Match the animal to its baby. The first one is done for you.

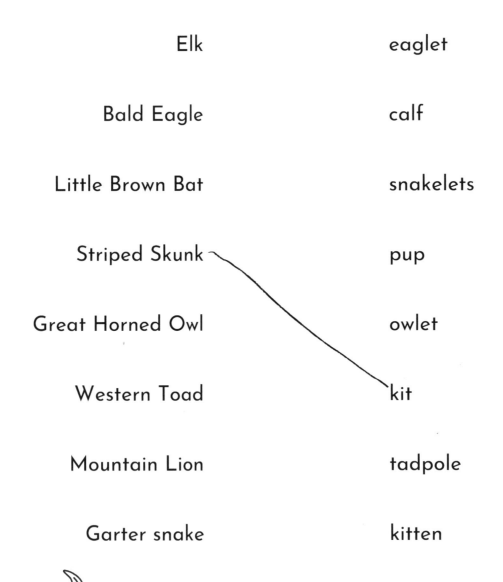

Elk	eaglet
Bald Eagle	calf
Little Brown Bat	snakelets
Striped Skunk	pup
Great Horned Owl	owlet
Western Toad	kit
Mountain Lion	tadpole
Garter snake	kitten

Exploring the Dark Sky

This park is a popular destination for stargazing. You may see stars in the night sky here that you may not see at home. Why do you think that is?

For all of time, people from across the world have looked at the night sky and seen images in the stars. They created stories about groups of stars, also called constellations. Create your own constellation that you see in the starfield below!

What is your constellation named?

The Perfect Picnic Spot

Fill in the blanks on this page without looking at the full story. Once you have each line filled out, use the words you've chosen to complete the story on the next page.

EMOTION _____

FOOD _____

SOMETHING SWEET _____

STORE _____

MODE OF TRANSPORTATION _____

NOUN _____

SOMETHING ALIVE _____

SAUCE _____

PLURAL VEGETABLES _____

ADJECTIVE _____

PLURAL BODY PART _____

ANIMAL _____

PLURAL FRUIT _____

PLACE _____

SOMETHING TALL _____

COLOR _____

ADJECTIVE _____

NOUN _____

A DIFFERENT ANIMAL _____

FAMILY MEMBER #1 _____

FAMILY MEMBER #2 _____

VERB THAT ENDS IN -ING _____

A DIFFERENT FOOD _____

The Perfect Picnic Spot

Use the words from the previous page to complete a silly story.

When my family suggested having our lunch at the Lewis Lake Picnic area, I

was _ _ _ _ _ _ _ _. I love eating my _ _ _ _ _ _ outside! I knew we had picked up a
      EMOTION   FOOD

box of _ _ _ _ _ _ from the _ _ _ _ _ _ _ _ for after lunch, my favorite. We drove up
    SOMETHING SWEET   STORE

to the area and I jumped out of the _ _ _ _ _ _ _ _. "I will find the perfect spot for
                           MODE OF TRANSPORTATION

a picnic!" I grabbed a _ _ _ _ _ _ for us to sit on, and I ran off. I passed a picnic
                NOUN

table, but it was covered with _ _ _ _ _ _ _ _ so we couldn't sit there. The next
                SOMETHING ALIVE

picnic table looked okay, but there were smears of _ _ _ _ _ _ _ and pieces of
                          SAUCE

_ _ _ _ _ _ _ _ everywhere. The people that were there before must have been
PLURAL VEGETABLES

_ _ _ _ _ _! I gritted my _ _ _ _ _ _ _ together and kept walking down the path,
ADJECTIVE   PLURAL BODY PART

determined to find the perfect spot. I wanted a table with a good view of the

lake. Why was this so hard? If we were lucky, I might even get to see _ _ _ _ _ _
                               ANIMAL

eating some _ _ _ _ _ _ on the water's edge. They don't have those in _ _ _ _ _ _ _
      PLURAL FRUIT   PLACE

where I am from. I walked down a little hill and there it was, the perfect spot!

The trees towered overhead and looked as tall as _ _ _ _ _ _ _ _. The patch of
                         SOMETHING TALL

grass was a beautiful _ _ _ _ _ _ color. The _ _ _ _ _ _ flowers were growing on
           COLOR   ADJECTIVE

the side of a _ _ _ _ _ _ _. I looked across the lake edge and even saw a
          NOUN

_ _ _ _ _ _ _ _ on the edge of a rock. I looked back to see my _ _ _ _ _ _ _ _ _ and
DIFFERENT ANIMAL   FAMILY MEMBER #1

_ _ _ _ _ _ _ _ _ _ _ _ _ _ a picnic basket. "I hope you brought plenty of
FAMILY MEMBER #2   VERB THAT ENDS IN ING

_ _ _ _ _ _ _, I'm starving!"
A DIFFERENT FOOD

29

Hike to a Geyser

start here

DID YOU KNOW?
There nearly 500 geysers in Yellowstone National Park.

Old Faithful Inn Word Search

The Old Faithful Inn is a hotel located near the famous Old Faithful Geyser. The hotel is made from logs from Lodgepole Pine trees and is considered to be one of the great national park lodges of the west. The rustic-style lodge was designed by architect Robert Reamer. Since opening in 1904, it has welcomed guests such as President Warren Harding, President Calvin Coolidge, and President Franklin Roosevelt.

1. lodge
2. Robert Reamer
3. hotel
4. rustic
5. geyser
6. inn
7. logs
8. sleep
9. lodgepole
10. Old Faithful
11. overnight
12. rest
13. parkitechture
14. landmark

```
F M R H O T E L B S T O N G S
E O I D P W A O E R B C N E N
G W C N M P S G B A E I K Y G
R J T R N R I S L T C T U S K
O V E R N I G H T L A S W E P
V J D S R T D E A N U L R L
P L P U A A R D B N T R S N O
R U M A R L C O L D E R I R D
A F A T M D L E S M U R W E G
F H M U L E T Y A A N R O V E
T T P L O D G E P R C T E O P
E I A H I C R G S K I U A K O
R A O W I T T O L B T R M C L
S F P A R K I T E C H T U R E
S D U E E R I D E R T N A L E
I L B V V N H S P T R A Q O R
O O O T G D E E O O O R V W S
R E S T K C A B I N S O H E M
```

National Park Service rustic, or "Parkitecture" is a style of architecture that developed in the 1900s. The United States National Park Service (NPS) makes an effort to create buildings that blend well with the natural environment.

Leave No Trace Quiz

Leave No Trace is a concept that helps people make decisions during outdoor recreation that protects the environment. There are seven principles that guide us when we spend time outdoors, whether you are in a national park or not. Are you an expert in Leave No Trace? Take this quiz and find out!

1. How can you plan ahead and prepare to ensure you have the best experience you can in the national park?
   a. Make sure you stop by the ranger station for a map and to ask about current conditions.
   b. Just wing it! You will know the best trail when you see it.
   c. Stick to your plan, even if conditions change. You traveled a long way to get here, and you should stick to your plan.

2. What is an example of traveling on a durable surface?
   a. Walking only on the designated path.
   b. Walking on the grass that borders the trail if the trail is very muddy.
   c. Taking a shortcut if you can find one since it means you will be walking less.

3. Why should you dispose of waste properly?
   a. You don't need to. Park rangers love to pick up the trash you leave behind.
   b. You actually should leave your leftovers behind, because animals will eat them. It is important to make sure they aren't hungry.
   c. So that other peoples' experiences of the park are not impacted by you leaving your waste behind.

4. How can you best follow the concept "leave what you find"?
   a. Take only a small rock or leaf to remember your trip.
   b. Take pictures, but leave any physical items where they are.
   c. Leave everything you find, unless it may be rare like an arrowhead, then it is okay to take.

5. What is not a good example of minimizing campfire impacts?
   a. Only having a campfire in a pre-existing campfire ring.
   b. Checking in with current conditions when you consider making a campfire.
   c. Building a new campfire ring in a location that has a better view.

6. What is a poor example of respecting wildlife?
   a. Building squirrel houses out of rocks so the squirrels have a place to live.
   b. Stay far away from wildlife and give them plenty of space.
   c. Reminding your grown-ups to not drive too fast in animal habitats while visiting the park.

7. How can you show consideration of other visitors?
   a. Play music on your speaker so other people at the campground can enjoy it.
   b. Wear headphones on the trail if you choose to listen to music.
   c. Make sure to yell "Hello!" to every animal you see at top volume.

Park Poetry

America's parks inspire art of all kinds. Painters, sculptors, photographers, writers, and artists of all mediums have taken inspiration from natural beauty. They have turned their inspiration into great works.

Use this space to write your own poem about the park. Think about what you have experienced or seen. Use descriptive language to create an acrostic poem. This type of poem has the first letter of each line spell out another word. Create an acrostic that spells out the word "Bison."

B _____

I _____

S _____

O _____

N _____

Big bison

In the prairie

Sunshine

Overhead

Noble creature

Boiling water

I see hot springs

so colorful

Orange and red

Never stop steaming

33

Being Respectful

Rangers need your help! Some people toss their trash where they shouldn't, create graffiti, or take artifacts when they visit Yellowstone National Park. Create a poster to help show other visitors how to be respectful in the space below.

Catch a Fish in the Madison River

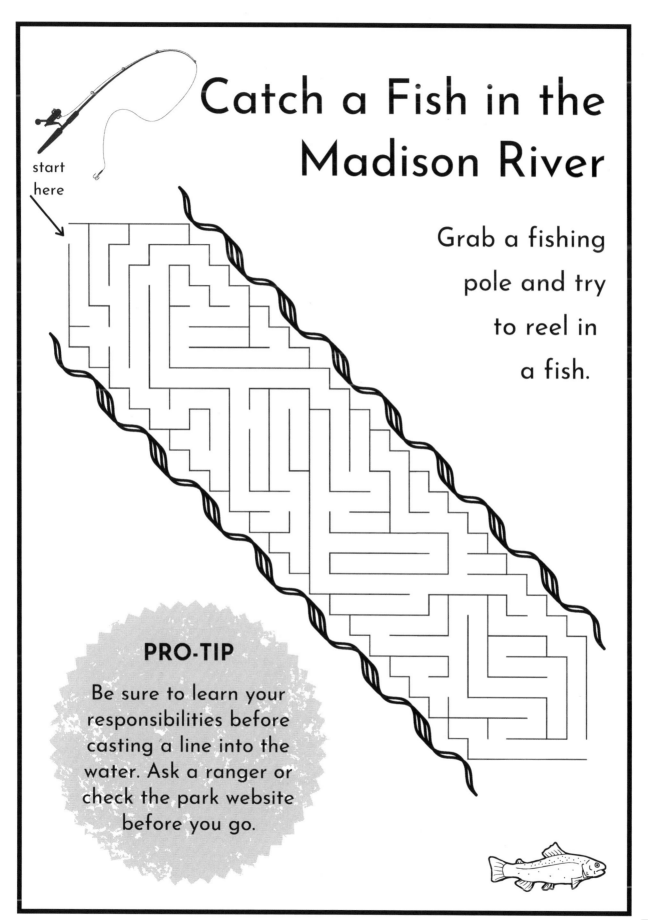

start here

Grab a fishing pole and try to reel in a fish.

PRO-TIP

Be sure to learn your responsibilities before casting a line into the water. Ask a ranger or check the park website before you go.

Stacking Rocks

Have you ever seen stacks of rocks while hiking in national parks? Do you know what they are or what they mean? These rock piles are called cairns and often mark hiking routes in parks. Every park has a different way to maintain trails and cairns. However, they all have the same rule: If you come across a cairn, do not disturb it.

Color the cairn and the rules to remember.

1. Do not tamper with cairns.

If a cairn is tampered with or an unauthorized one is built, then future visitors may become disoriented or even lost.

2. Do not build unauthorized cairns.

Moving rocks disturbs the soil and makes the area more prone to erosion. Disturbing rocks can disturb fragile plants.

3. Do not add to existing cairns.

Authorized cairns are carefully designed. Adding to them can actually cause them to collapse.

Decoding Using American Sign Language

American Sign Language, also called ASL for short, is a language that many people who are deaf or hard of hearing use to communicate. People use ASL to communicate with their hands. Did you know people from all over the country and world travel to national parks? You may hear people speaking other languages. You might also see people using ASL. Use the American Manual Alphabet chart to decode some national parks facts.

This was the first national park to be established:

This is the biggest national park in the US:

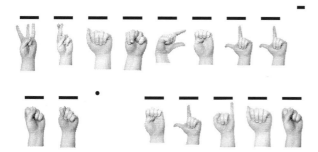

This is the most visited national park:

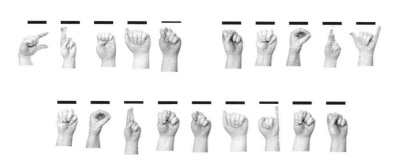

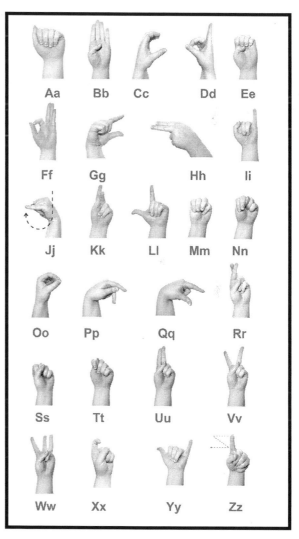

Hint: Pay close attention to the position of the thumb!

 Try it! Using the chart, try to make the letters of the alphabet with your hand. What is the hardest letter to make? Can you spell out your name? Show a friend or family member and have them watch you spell out the name of the national park you are in.

Go Horseback Riding at Swan Lake Flat

Help find the horse's lost shoe!

start here

DID YOU KNOW?

Horseback riding is a popular activity in Yellowstone National Park. There are many trails that you can take horses for day trips.

Butterflies of Yellowstone

Dozens of species of butterflies and moths live in Yellowstone National Park. Their wingspan size varies, as do the patterns on their wings. Design your own butterfly below. Make sure the wings are symmetrical, meaning both sides match.

A Hike at Grand Prismatic

Fill in the blanks on this page without looking at the full story. Once you have each line filled out, use the words you've chosen to complete the story on the next page.

ADJECTIVE --

SOMETHING TO EAT --

SOMETHING TO DRINK --------------------------------------

NOUN ---

ARTICLE OF CLOTHING -------------------------------------

BODY PART --

VERB ---

ANIMAL ---

SAME TYPE OF FOOD ---------------------------------------

ADJECTIVE --

SAME ANIMAL --

VERB THAT ENDS IN "ED" ----------------------------------

NUMBER ---

A DIFFERENT NUMBER -------------------------------------

SOMETHING THAT FLIES -----------------------------------

LIGHT SOURCE ---

PLURAL NOUN --

FAMILY MEMBER --

YOUR NICKNAME --

A Hike at Grand Prismatic

Use the words from the previous page to complete a silly story.

I went for a hike at Grand Prismatic Hot Spring today. In my favorite

_____ backpack, I made sure to pack a map so I wouldn't get lost. I also
ADJECTIVE

threw in an extra _____ just in case I got hungry and a bottle of
SOMETHING TO EAT

_____. I put on my _____ spray, and a tied a
SOMETHING TO DRINK   NOUN

_____ around my _____, in case it gets chilly. I started to
ARTICLE OF CLOTHING   BODY PART

_____ down the path. As soon as I turned the corner, I came face to face
VERB

with a(n) _____. I think it was as startled as I was! What should I do? I
ANIMAL

had to think fast! Should I give it some of my _____? No. I had to
SAME TYPE OF FOOD

remember what the _____ ranger told me. "If you see one, back away
ADJECTIVE

slowly and try not to scare it." Soon enough, the _____
SAME ANIMAL

_____ away. The coast was clear. _____ hours later, I finally got to
VERB THAT ENDS IN ED   NUMBER

the lookout. I felt like I could see for a _____ miles. I took a picture of a
A DIFFERENT NUMBER

_____ so I could always remember this moment. As I was putting my
NOUN

camera away, a _____ flew by, reminding me that it was almost
SOMETHING THAT FLIES

nighttime. I turned on my _____ and headed back. I could hear the
LIGHT SOURCE

_____ singing their evening song. Just as I was getting tired, I saw
PLURAL INSECT

my _____ and our tent. "Welcome back _____! How was your
FAMILY MEMBER   NICKNAME

hike?"

41

Protecting the Park

When you visit national parks, it is important to leave the park the way you found it. Did you know that the national parks get hundreds of millions of visitors every year? We can only protect national parks for future visitors to enjoy if everyone does their part. The choices that each visitor makes when visiting the park have a big impact all together.

Read each line below. Write a sentence or draw a picture to show the impacts these changes would make on the park.

What would happen if every visitor fed the wild animals?

What would happen if every visitor picked a flower?

What would happen if every visitor took home a few rocks?

What would happen if every visitor wrote or carved their name on the rocks or trees?

Let's Go Camping
Word Search

Words may be horizontal, vertical, or diagonal and they might be backward!

1. tent
2. camp stove
3. sleeping bag
4. bug spray
5. sunscreen
6. map
7. flashlight
8. pillow
9. lantern
10. ice
11. snacks
12. smores
13. water
14. first aid kit
15. chair
16. cards
17. books
18. games
19. trail
20. hat

```
D P P I L L O W D B T E A C I
E O A D P R E A A M B R C A N
P W C A M P S T O V E I H X G
R A H S G E L E B E E D A P S
E L B U G S P R A Y N G I E A
S I A H G C I C N N M E R C N
C W N L A F I R S K O O B F K
M T A E M I L E L H M R W L J
T A P R E A O R E S L B A A B
S M P A S R R T E N T L U S C
C E A I I R C G P E I U J H A
S S N A C K S S I M O K I L R
I J R S F O I S N J R A Q I D
C Y E T L E V E G U O R V G S
E W T A K C A B B S S O H H M
X J N F I R S T A I D K I T T
U A A E S S E N G E T P V A B
C J L I A R T D N A M A H A S
```

All in the Day of a Park Ranger

Park Rangers are hardworking individuals dedicated to protecting our parks, monuments, museums, and more. They take care of the natural and cultural resources for future generations. Rangers also help protect the visitors of the park. Their responsibilities are broad and they work both with the public and behind the scenes.

What have you seen park rangers do? Use your knowledge of the duties of park rangers to fill out a typical daily schedule, one activity for each hour. Feel free to make up your own, but some examples of activities are provided on the right. Read carefully, not all of the example activities are befitting a ranger!

6 am	Lead a sunrise hike
7 am	
8 am	
9 am	
10 am	
11 am	
12 pm	Enjoy a lunch break outside
1 pm	
2 pm	
3 pm	
4 pm	Teach visitors about the geology of the mountains
5 pm	
6 pm	
7 pm	
8 pm	
9 pm	

- feed the bald eagles
- build trails for visitors to enjoy
- throw rocks off the side of the mountain
- rescue lost hikers
- study animal behavior
- record air quality data
- answer questions at the visitor center
- pick wildflowers
- pick up litter
- share marshmallows with squirrels
- repair handrails
- lead a class on a field trip
- catch frogs and make them race
- lead people on educational hikes
- write articles for the park website
- protect the river from pollution
- remove non-native plants from the park
- study how climate change is affecting the park
- give a talk about mountain lions
- lead a program for campers on salmon

If you were a park ranger, which of the above tasks would you enjoy most?

_____

_____

44

Draw Yourself as a Park Ranger

The Fish at Yellowstone

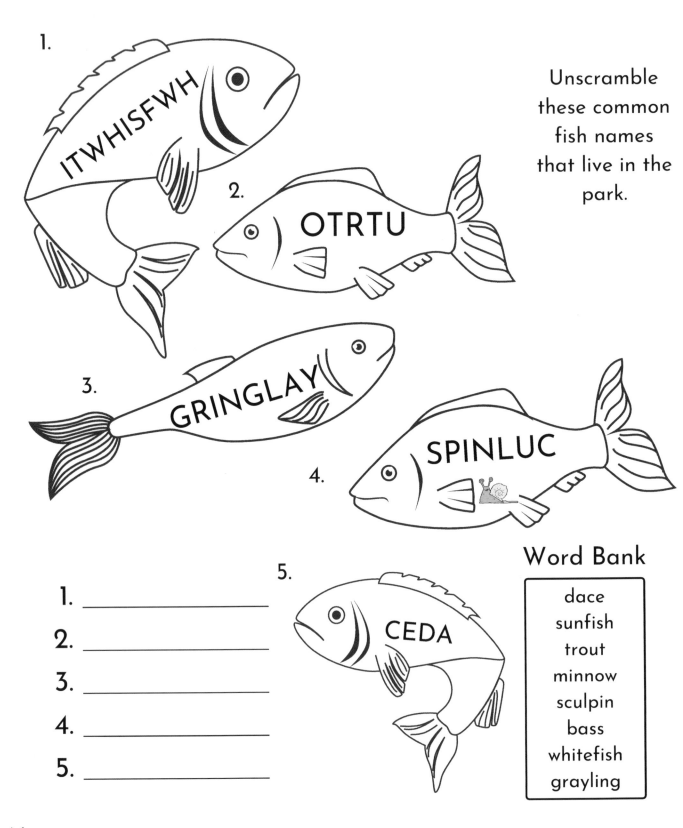

1. ITWHISFWH

2. OTRTU

3. GRINGLAY

4. SPINLUC

5. CEDA

Unscramble these common fish names that live in the park.

1. _____
2. _____
3. _____
4. _____
5. _____

Word Bank

dace
sunfish
trout
minnow
sculpin
bass
whitefish
grayling

Amphibians

One species of salamanders, two kinds of toads, and two kinds of frogs live in Yellowstone National Park. Frogs and toads both spend the beginning of their lives the same way, as tadpoles. Tadpoles hatch from eggs in water, usually in springs or pools of water.

Both frogs and toads are amphibians. Salamanders are amphibians too. Color the amphibians below.

Photobook

Draw some pictures of
things you saw in the park.

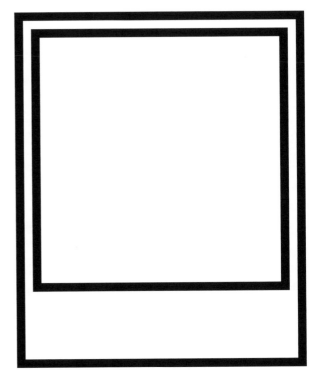

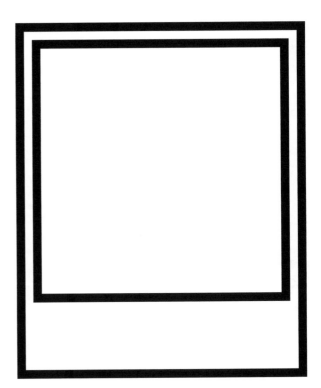

Design a Badge

Imagine you've been hired to create a badge that will be for sale in the national park gift shop. Your badge will be a souvenir for visitors to remember their trip to the park.

Consider adding a plant or animal that lives here, or include a famous place in the park or activity that you can do while visiting.

63 National Parks

How many other national parks have you been to? Which one do you want to visit next? Note that some of these parks fall on the border of more than one state, you may check it off more than once!

Alaska
- [ ] Denali National Park
- [ ] Gates of the Arctic National Park
- [ ] Glacier Bay National Park
- [ ] Katmai National Park
- [ ] Kenai Fjords National Park
- [ ] Kobuk Valley National Park
- [ ] Lake Clark National Park
- [ ] Wrangell-St. Elias National Park

American Samoa
- [ ] National Park of American Samoa

Arizona
- [ ] Grand Canyon National Park
- [ ] Petrified Forest National Park
- [ ] Saguaro National Park

Arkansas
- [ ] Hot Springs National Park

California
- [ ] Channel Islands National Park
- [ ] Death Valley National Park
- [ ] Joshua Tree National Park
- [ ] Kings Canyon National Park
- [ ] Lassen Volcanic National Park
- [ ] Pinnacles National Park
- [ ] Redwood National Park
- [ ] Sequoia National Park
- [ ] Yosemite National Park

Colorado
- [ ] Black Canyon of the Gunnison National Park
- [ ] Great Sand Dunes National Park
- [ ] Mesa Verde National Park
- [ ] Rocky Mountain National Park

Florida
- [ ] Biscayne National Park
- [ ] Dry Tortugas National Park
- [ ] Everglades National Park

Hawaii
- [ ] Haleakala National Park
- [ ] Hawai'i Volcanoes National Park

Idaho
- [ ] Yellowstone National Park

Kentucky
- [ ] Mammoth Cave National Park

Indiana
- [ ] Indiana Dunes National Park

Maine
- [ ] Acadia National Park

Michigan
- [ ] Isle Royale National Park

Minnesota
- [ ] Voyageurs National Park

Missouri
- [ ] Gateway Arch National Park

Montana
- [ ] Glacier National Park
- [ ] Yellowstone National Park

Nevada
- [ ] Death Valley National Park
- [ ] Great Basin National Park

New Mexico
- [ ] Carlsbad Caverns National Park
- [ ] White Sands National Park

North Dakota
- [ ] Theodore Roosevelt National Park

North Carolina
- [ ] Great Smoky Mountains National Park

Ohio
- [ ] Cuyahoga Valley National Park

Oregon
- [ ] Crater Lake National Park

South Carolina
- [ ] Congaree National Park

South Dakota
- [ ] Badlands National Park
- [ ] Wind Cave National Park

Tennessee
- [ ] Great Smoky Mountains National Park

Texas
- [ ] Big Bend National Park
- [ ] Guadalupe Mountains National Park

Utah
- [ ] Arches National Park
- [ ] Bryce Canyon National Park
- [ ] Canyonlands National Park
- [ ] Capitol Reef National Park
- [ ] Zion National Park

Virgin Islands
- [ ] Virgin Islands National Park

Virginia
- [ ] Shenandoah National Park

Washington
- [ ] Mount Rainier National Park
- [ ] North Cascades National Park
- [ ] Olympic National Park

West Virginia
- [ ] New River Gorge National Park

Wyoming
- [ ] Grand Teton National Park
- [ ] Yellowstone National Park

Other National Parks

Besides Yellowstone National Park, there are 62 other diverse and beautiful national parks across the United States. Try your hand at this crossword. If you need help, look at the previous page for some hints.

Down

1. State where Acadia National Park is located
2. This national park has the Spanish word for turtle in it.
3. Number of national parks in Alaska
5. This national park has some of the hottest temperatures in the world.
6. This national park is the only one in Idaho.
7. This toothsome creature can be famously found in Everglades National Park.
8. Only president with a national park named for them

Across

4. This state has the most national parks.
9. This park has some of the newest land in the US, caused by volcanic eruptions.
10. This park has the deepest lake in the United States.
11. This color shows up in the name of a national park in California.
12. This national park deserves a gold medal.

Which National Park Will You Go to Next?
Word Search

1. Zion
2. Big Bend
3. Glacier
4. Olympic
5. Sequoia
6. Bryce
7. Mesa Verde
8. Biscayne
9. Wind Cave
10. Great Basin
11. Katmai
12. Yellowstone
13. Voyageurs
14. Arches
15. Badlands
16. Denali
17. Glacier Bay
18. Hot Springs

```
F  M  M  E  S  A  V  E  R  D  E  B  N  E  Y
E  A  B  I  G  B  E  N  D  E  S  A  S  E  M
Y  L  I  C  A  L  O  Y  N  E  E  D  L  T  G
D  M  G  A  S  S  A  U  C  N  R  L  U  E  R
C  E  L  I  I  T  S  C  R  E  O  A  A  K  E
S  N  A  W  Y  E  E  O  I  W  T  N  A  C  A
G  I  C  H  A  A  Q  C  S  E  M  D  N  S  T
N  O  I  Z  P  R  U  T  I  M  R  S  N  E  B
I  W  E  L  M  P  O  N  B  W  E  B  K  H  A
R  J  R  F  D  N  I  F  L  I  H  B  U  C  S
P  A  B  E  E  S  A  N  E  S  O  P  W  R  I
S  J  A  E  N  Y  A  C  S  I  B  A  U  A  N
T  C  Y  I  A  D  O  H  H  Y  M  E  A  L  R
O  T  A  T  L  M  L  E  S  E  G  R  W  R  J
H  S  T  O  I  K  A  T  M  A  I  R  O  P  B
I  C  H  U  R  C  O  L  Y  M  P  I  C  O  U
O  Y  G  T  S  D  E  O  S  B  R  Y  C  E  T
W  I  N  D  C  A  V  E  I  N  R  O  H  E  M
```

52

Field Notes

Spend some time to reflect on your trip to Yellowstone National Park. Your field notes will help you remember the things you experienced. Use the space below to write about your day.

While I was at Yellowstone National Park...

I saw:

_____

_____

_____

_____

_____

I heard:

_____

_____

_____

_____

I felt:

_____

_____

Draw a picture of your favorite thing in the park.

I wondered:

_____

_____

_____

_____

_____

ANSWER KEY

National Park Emblem Answers

1. This represents all plants. **Sequoia Tree**

2. This represents all animals. **Bison**

3. This symbol represents the landscapes. **Mountains**

4. This represents the waters protected by the park service. **Water**

5. This represents the historical and archeological values. **Arrowhead**

Jumbles Answers

1. BOATING

2. HIKING

3. BIRDING

4. CAMPING

5. PICNICKING

6. SIGHTSEEING

7. SNOWSHOEING

Go Birdwatching at Swan Lake Flatts

start here

Answers: Who lives here?

Here are seven animals that live in the park.
Use the word bank to fill in the clues below.

WORD BANK: WESTERN TOAD, PYGMY OWL, RIVER OTTER, MOOSE,
BISON, BADGER, GOLDEN EAGLE

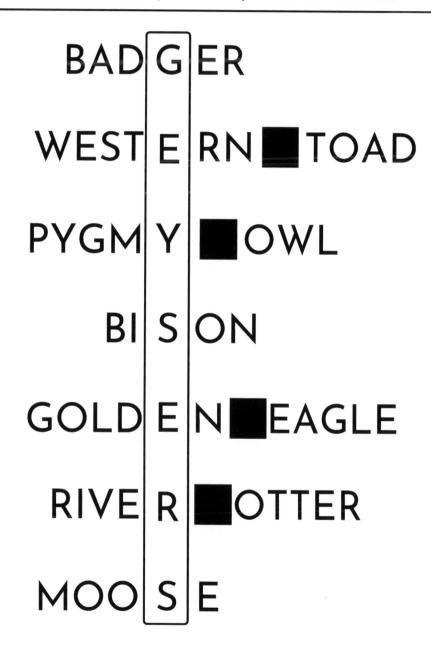

BAD**G**ER

WEST**E**RN ■ TOAD

PYGM**Y** ■ OWL

BI**S**ON

GOLD**E**N ■ EAGLE

RIVE**R** ■ OTTER

MOO**S**E

Find the Match!
Common Names and Latin Names

Match the common name to the scientific name for each animal. The first one is done for you. Use clues on the page before and after this one to complete the matches.

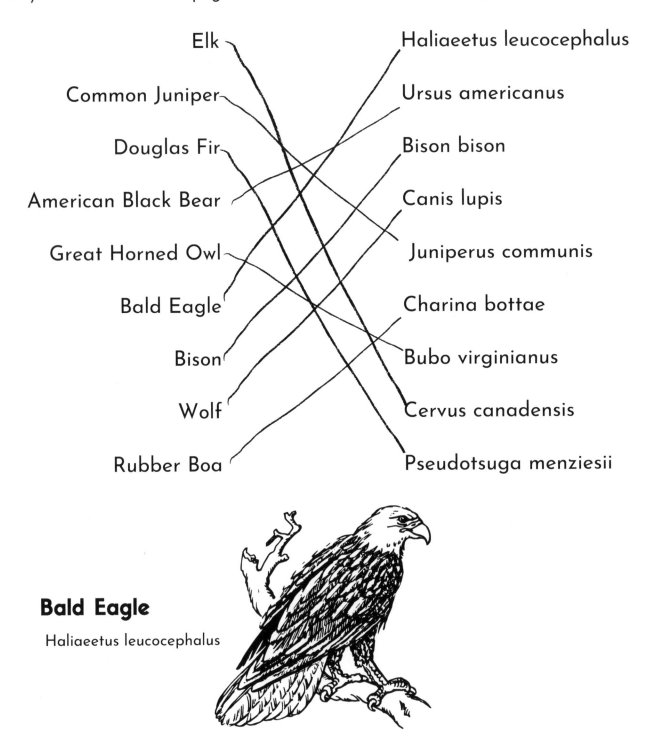

Elk

Common Juniper

Douglas Fir

American Black Bear

Great Horned Owl

Bald Eagle

Bison

Wolf

Rubber Boa

Haliaeetus leucocephalus

Ursus americanus

Bison bison

Canis lupis

Juniperus communis

Charina bottae

Bubo virginianus

Cervus canadensis

Pseudotsuga menziesii

Bald Eagle

Haliaeetus leucocephalus

Answers: The Ten Essentials

The ten essentials is a list of things that are important to have when you go for longer hikes. If you go on a hike to the <u>backcountry</u>, it is especially important that you have everything you need in case of an emergency. If you get lost or something unforeseen happens, it is good to be prepared to survive until help finds you.

The ten essentials list was developed in the 1930s by an outdoors group called the Mountaineers. Over time and technological advancements, this list has evolved. Can you identify all the things on the current list? Circle each of the "essentials" and cross out everything that doesn't make the cut.

Backcountry- a remote undeveloped rural area.

Yellowstone Word Search

Words may be horizontal, vertical, or diagonal
and they might be backward!

1. Old Faithful
2. squirrel
3. coyote
4. Roosevelt Arch
5. mud pots
6. Montana
7. geyser
8. Wyoming
9. Idaho
10. bison
11. boardwalk
12. Boiling River
13. hot spring
14. lodge
15. camping
16. wolves
17. travertine
18. hydrothermal

```
H M R E G N I M O Y W O M D M
E Y I E P W A T O R O R O A R
O L D F A I T H F U L I N G O
S O H R O D I C L T V B T H O
A D E C O Y O T E S E P A G S
V G D S L T G H B I S O N E E
P E P O V E H S B G T A A N V
E L M A R Y O E E T E T I R E
R T P T M O T Y R R E L W C L
K S Y U H E S R T M N A S A T
L G R A F E P D R C A N T M A
A N D H R F R G R K H L O P R
W I E W I A I O I F T I P I C
D P B H R S N N N A M C D N H
R M N L E R G D S C T N U G O
A S Q U I R R E L E R A M E N
O C R T R A V E R T I N E W D
B O I L I N G R I V E R A D M
```

60

Answers: Find the Match!
What are Baby Animals Called?

Match the animal to its baby. The first one is done for you.

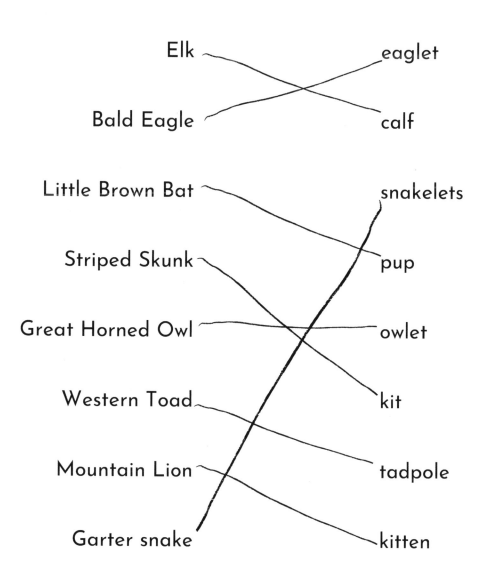

Elk   eaglet

Bald Eagle   calf

Little Brown Bat   snakelets

Striped Skunk   pup

Great Horned Owl   owlet

Western Toad   kit

Mountain Lion   tadpole

Garter snake   kitten

Hike to a Geyser

start here →

DID YOU KNOW?

There nearly 500 geysers in Yellowstone National Park.

Old Faithful Inn Word Search

The Old Faithful Inn is a hotel located near the famous Old Faithful Geyser. The hotel is made from logs from Lodgepole Pine trees and is considered to be one of the great national park lodges of the west. The rustic-style lodge was designed by architect Robert Reamer. Since opening in 1904, it has welcomed guests such as President Warren Harding, President Calvin Coolidge, and President Franklin Roosevelt.

1. lodge
2. Robert Reamer
3. hotel
4. rustic
5. geyser
6. inn
7. logs
8. sleep
9. lodgepole
10. Old Faithful
11. overnight
12. rest
13. parkitechture
14. landmark

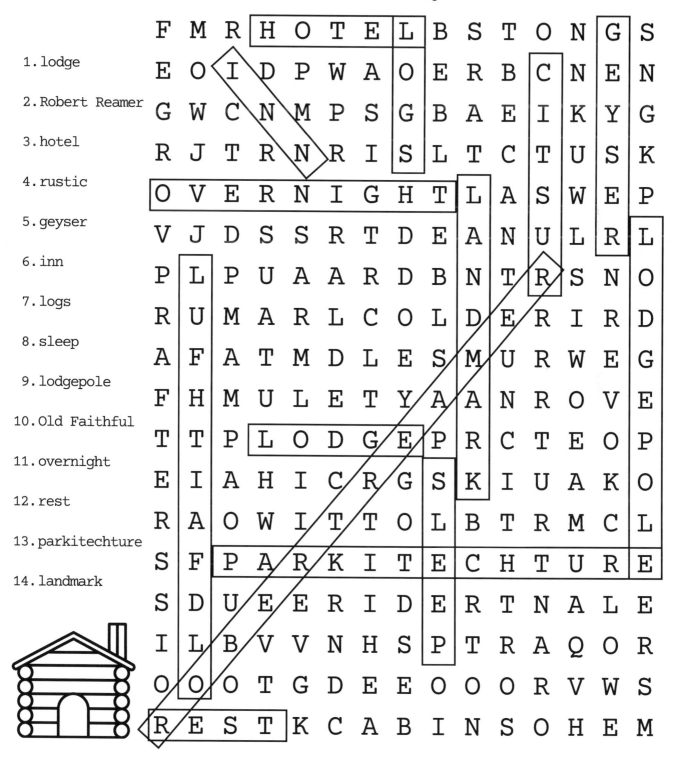

```
F M R H O T E L B S T O N G S
E O I D P W A O E R B C N E N
G W C N M P S G B A E I K Y G
R J T R N R I S L T C T U S K
O V E R N I G H T L A S W E P
V J D S S R T D E A N U L R L
P L P U A A R D B N T R S N O
R U M A R L C O L D E R I R D
A F A T M D L E S M U R W E G
F H M U L E T Y A A N R O V E
T T P L O D G E P R C T E O P
E I A H I C R G S K I U A K O
R A O W I T T O L B T R M C L
S F P A R K I T E C H T U R E
S D U E E R I D E R T N A L E
I L B V V N H S P T R A Q O R
O O O T G D E E O O R V W S
R E S T K C A B I N S O H E M
```

National Park Service rustic, or "Parkitecture" is a style of architecture that developed in the 1900s. The United States National Park Service (NPS) makes an effort to create buildings that blend well with the natural environment.

Answers: Leave No Trace Quiz

Leave No Trace is a concept that helps people make decisions during outdoor recreation that protects the environment. There are seven principles that guide us when we spend time outdoors, whether you are in a national park or not. Are you an expert in Leave No Trace? Take this quiz and find out!

1. How can you plan ahead and prepare to ensure you have the best experience you can in the National Park?
   A. Make sure you stop by the ranger station for a map and to ask about current conditions.
2. What is an example of traveling on a durable surface?
   A. Walking only on the designated path.
3. Why should you dispose of waste properly?
   C. So that other peoples' experiences of the park are not impacted by you leaving your waste behind.
4. How can you best follow the concept "leave what you find"?
   B. Take pictures but leave any physical items where they are.
5. What is not a good example of minimizing campfire impacts?
   C. Building a new campfire ring in a location that has a better view.
6. What is a poor example of respecting wildlife?
   A. Building squirrel houses out of rocks from the river so the squirrels have a place to live.
7. How can you show consideration of other visitors?
   B. Wear headphones on the trail if you choose to listen to music.

Solution: Catch a Fish in the Madison River

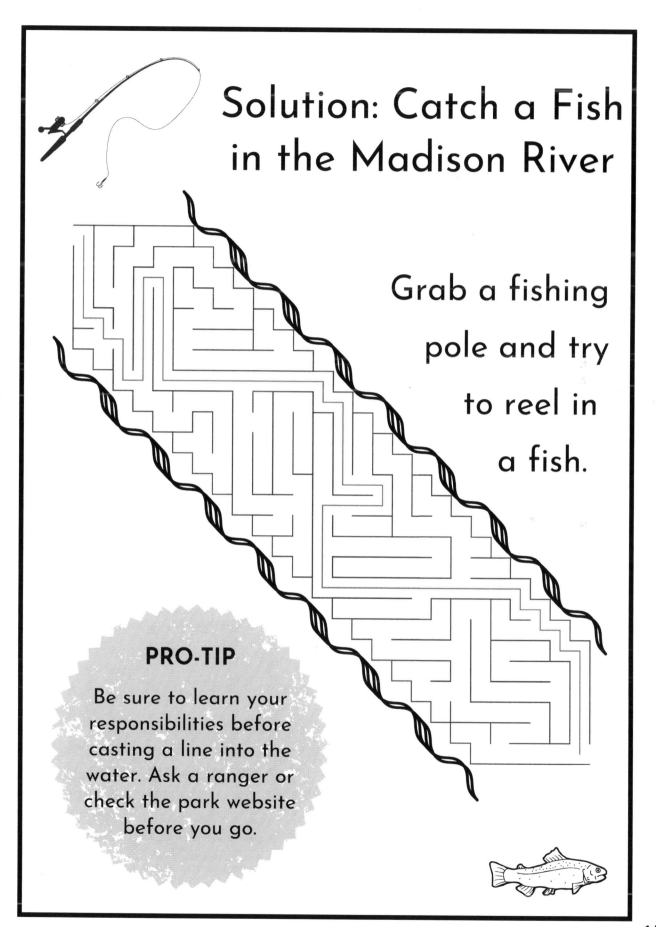

Grab a fishing pole and try to reel in a fish.

PRO-TIP

Be sure to learn your responsibilities before casting a line into the water. Ask a ranger or check the park website before you go.

Decoding Using American Sign Language

American Sign Language, also called ASL for short, is a language that many people who are deaf or hard of hearing use to communicate. People use ASL to communicate with their hands. Did you know people from all over the country and world travel to national parks? You may hear people speaking other languages. You might also see people using ASL. Use the American Manual Alphabet chart to decode some national parks facts.

This was the first national park to be established:

Y E L L O W S T O N E

This is the biggest national park in the US:

W R A N G E L L -
S T . E L I A S

This is the most visited national park:

G R E A T S M O K Y
M O U N T A I N S

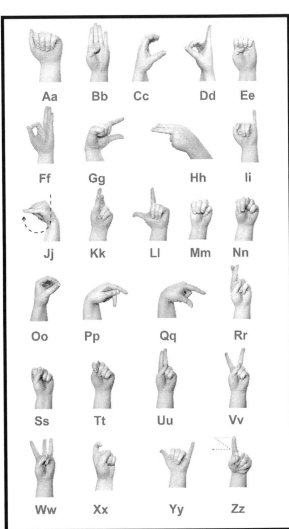

Hint: Pay close attention to the position of the thumb!

Try it! Using the chart, try to make the letters of the alphabet with your hand. What is the hardest letter to make? Can you spell out your name? Show a friend or family member and have them watch you spell out the name of the national park you are in.

Go Horseback Riding at Swan Lake Flat

Help find the horse's lost shoe!

start here

DID YOU KNOW?

Horseback riding is a popular activity in Yellowstone National Park. There are many trails that you can take horses for day trips.

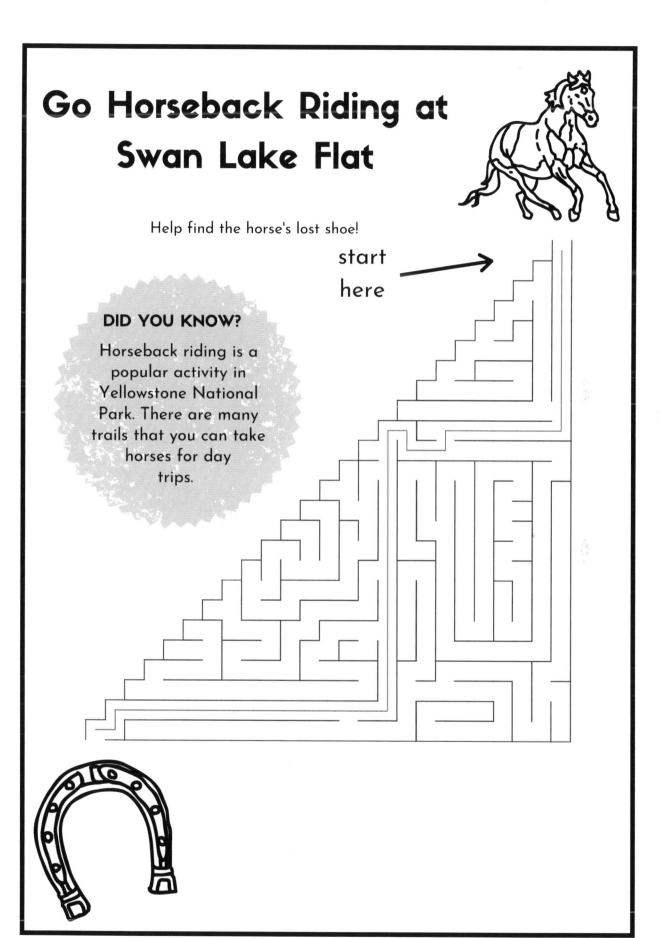

Let's Go Camping
Word Search

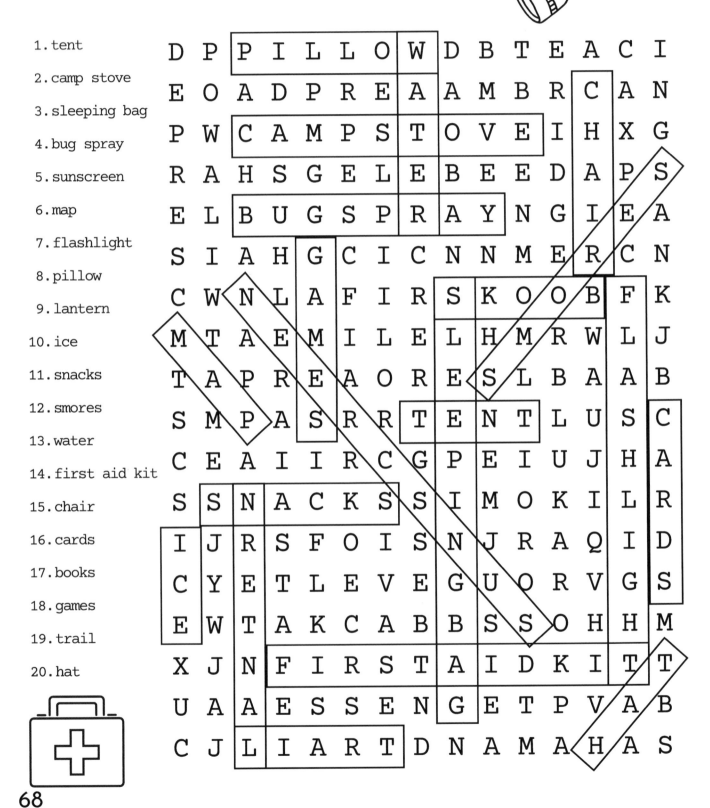

1. tent
2. camp stove
3. sleeping bag
4. bug spray
5. sunscreen
6. map
7. flashlight
8. pillow
9. lantern
10. ice
11. snacks
12. smores
13. water
14. first aid kit
15. chair
16. cards
17. books
18. games
19. trail
20. hat

D P P I L L O W D B T E A C I
E O A D P R E A A M B R C A N
P W C A M P S T O V E I H X G
R A H S G E L E B E E D A P S
E L B U G S P R A Y N G I E A
S I A H G C I C N N M E R C N
C W N L A F I R S K O O B F K
M T A E M I L E L H M R W L J
T A P R E A O R E S L B A A B
S M P A S R R T E N T L U S C
C E A I I R C G P E I U J H A
S S N A C K S S I M O K I L R
I J R S F O I S N J R A Q I D
C Y E T L E V E G U O R V G S
E W T A K C A B B S S O H H M
X J N F I R S T A I D K I T T
U A A E S S E N G E T P V A B
C J L I A R T D N A M A H A S

The Fish of Yellowstone

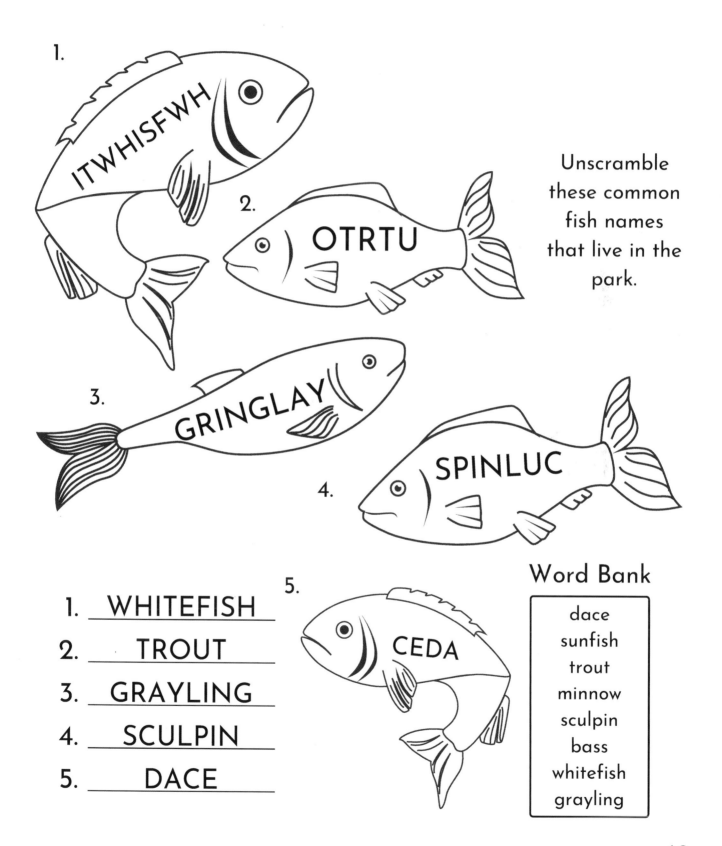

1. ITWHISFWH

2. OTRTU

3. GRINGLAY

4. SPINLUC

5. CEDA

Unscramble these common fish names that live in the park.

1. WHITEFISH
2. TROUT
3. GRAYLING
4. SCULPIN
5. DACE

Word Bank

dace
sunfish
trout
minnow
sculpin
bass
whitefish
grayling

Answers: Other National Parks

Down

1. State where Acadia National Park is located
2. This National Park has the Spanish word for turtle in it
3. Number of National Parks in Alaska
5. This National Park has some of the hottest temperatures in the world
6. This National Park is the only one in Idaho
7. This toothsome creature can be famously found in Everglades National Park
8. Only president with a national park named for them

Across

4. This state has the most National Parks
9. This park has some of the newest land in the US, caused by a volcanic eruption
10. This park has the deepest lake in the United States
11. This color shows up in the name of a National Park in California
12. This National Park deserves a gold medal

Answers: Where National Park Will You Go Next?

1. Zion
2. Big Bend
3. Glacier
4. Olympic
5. Sequoia
6. Bryce
7. Mesa Verde
8. Biscayne
9. Wind Cave
10. Great Basin
11. Katmai
12. Yellowstone
13. Voyageurs
14. Arches
15. Badlands
16. Denali
17. Glacier Bay
18. Hot Springs

```
F M M E S A V E R D E B N E Y
E A B I G B E N D E S A S E M
Y L I C A L O Y N E E D L T G
D M G A S S A U C N R L U E R
C E L I I T S C R E O A A K E
S N A W Y E E O I W T N A C A
G I C H A A Q C S E M D N S T
N O I Z P R U T I M R S N E B
I W E L M P O N B W E B K H A
R J R F D N I F L I H B U C S
P A B E E S A N E S O P W R I
S J A E N Y A C S I B A U A N
T C Y I A D O H H Y M E A L R
O T A T L M L E S E G R W R J
H S T O I K A T M A I R O P B
I C H U R C O L Y M P I C O U
O Y G T S D E O S B R Y C E T
W I N D C A V E I N R O H E M
```

LITTLE BISON
Press

Little Bison Press is an independent children's book publisher based in the Pacific Northwest. We promote exploration, conservation, and adventure through our books. Established in 2021, our passion for outside spaces and travel inspired the creation of Little Bison Press.

We seek to publish books that support children in learning about and caring for the natural places in our world.

To learn more, visit:
LittleBisonPress.com

Want more free games and activities? Visit our website!

Made in the USA
Middletown, DE
01 July 2022

68240863R00042